Emergency

Contents **Page**

written by Pam Holden

If an emergency happens near you, the first thing to do is to get help. Shout for somebody to help you. Run to the telephone, and call the emergency number.

You will be asked where you are,
so you must give your address.
Then you will be asked your name.
You need to tell what has happened,
so the right help can be sent to you.

An emergency can happen because of a fire. If you are in a building that has a fire, the first thing to do is to move! Get out!

Everybody needs to go outside before you call to get help. Firefighters will come quickly, and they will know what to do.

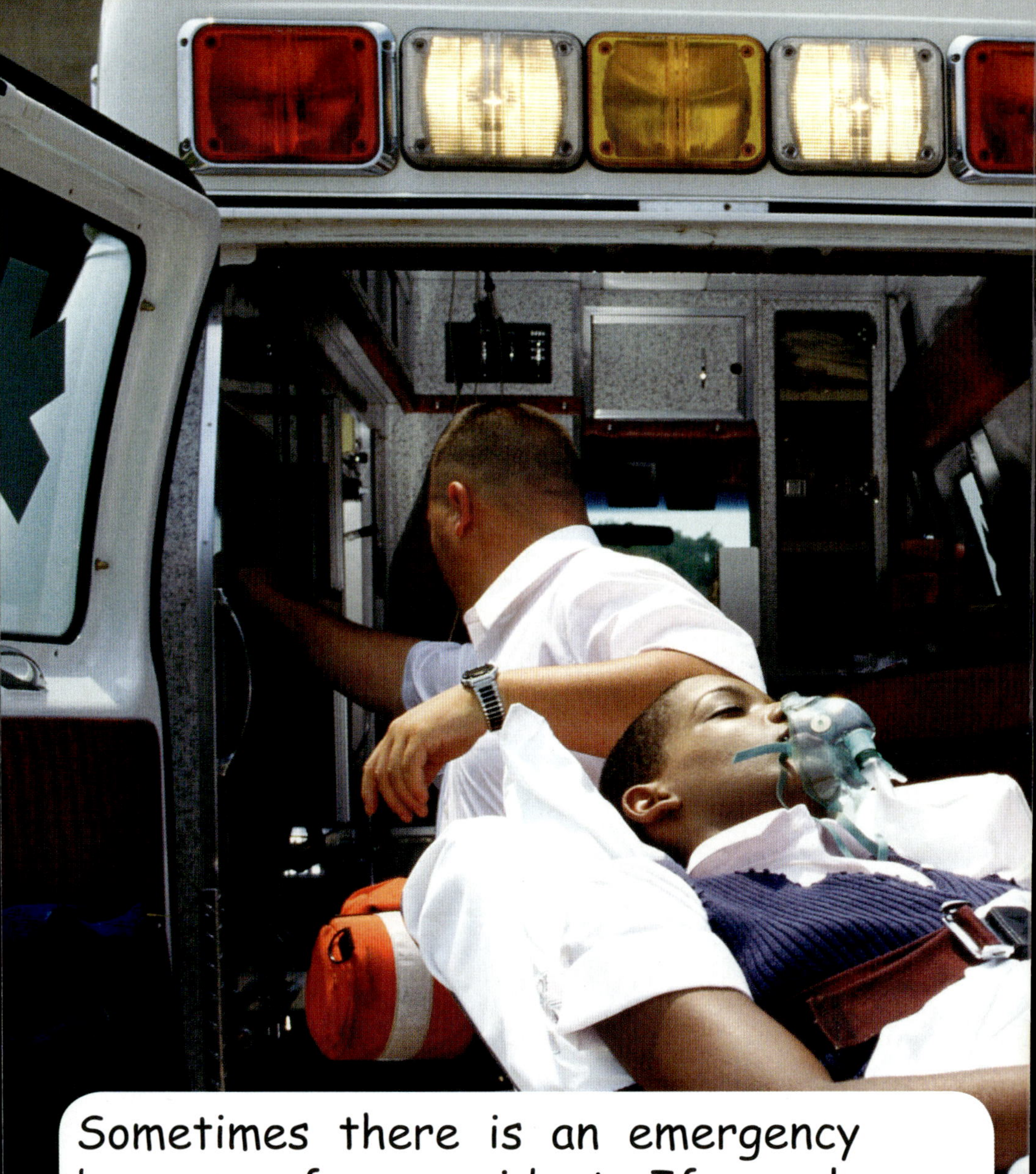

Sometimes there is an emergency because of an accident. If people are hurt, you need to call the emergency number on the phone right away.

You will be asked to tell what has happened, and how many people are hurt. An ambulance will soon be there with help.

There can be an emergency because of bad weather. If there is trouble from a storm or a flood, call for help.

flood

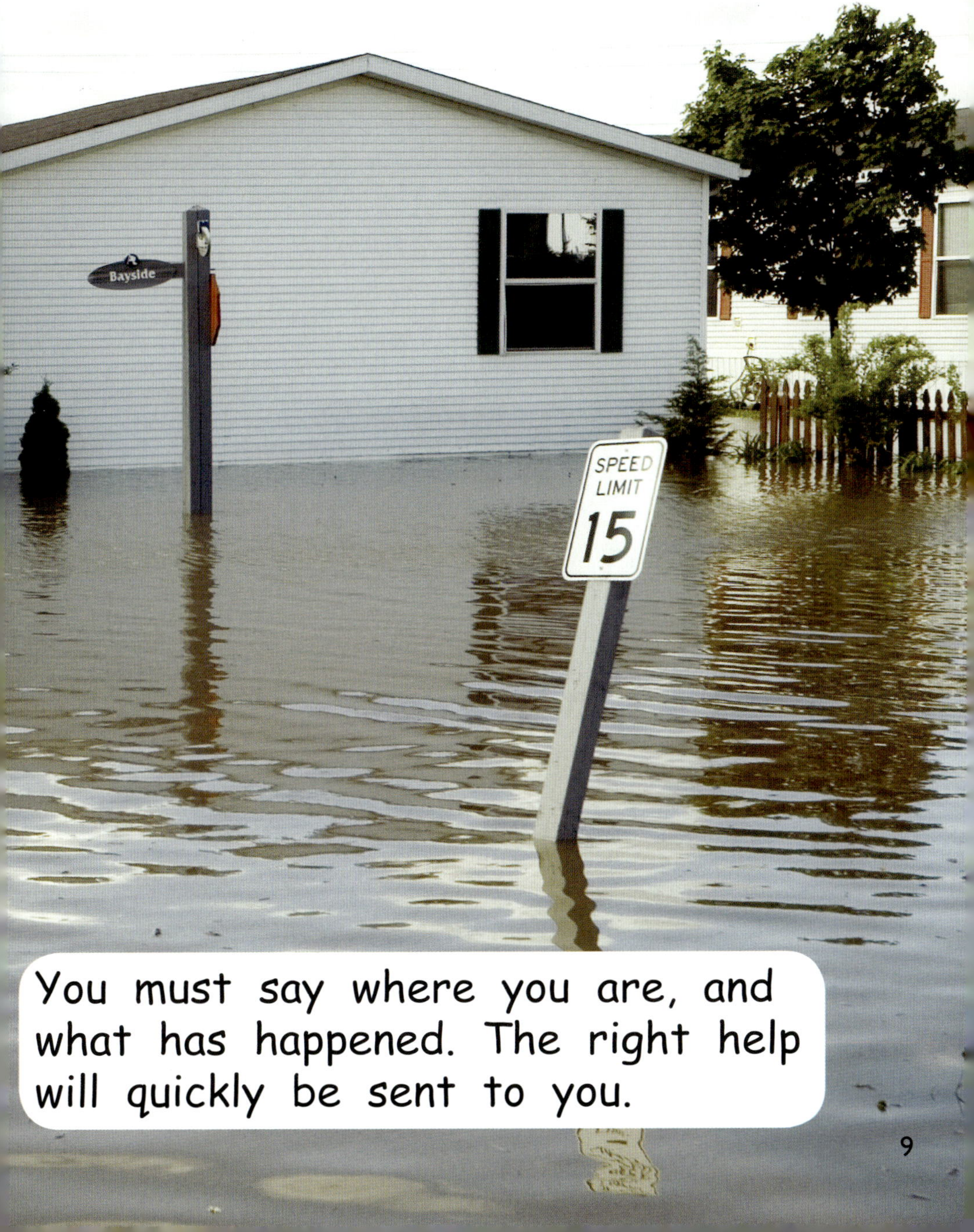

You must say where you are, and what has happened. The right help will quickly be sent to you.

An emergency can happen to people in boats, or swimming. If you see someone in trouble in the water, you must shout for help from somebody near you.

After that, you can get more help by using your phone. A rescue from the water must be quick.

surf lifesavers

Sometimes climbers get stuck on a mountain. Some people go into caves, then get stuck underground. If you see someone in trouble, you know who to call.

You must tell where the emergency is happening. A rescue team will bring whatever they need to help the people in trouble.

If you get lost in a city or a forest, you can call for help on a mobile phone. You will be asked what time you left home, and which way you went.

policeman
You must stay right where you are until helpers find you.

You may never have an emergency, but you know what to do if it happens. Remember the emergency phone number, so you will be able to help anybody who is in trouble.